The
UNITED
STATES
PRESIDENTS

Lyndon B.
JOHNSON

Megan M. Gunderson

Big Buddy Books
An Imprint of Abdo Publishing
abdopublishing.com

abdopublishing.com

Published by Abdo Publishing, a division of ABDO, PO Box 398166, Minneapolis, Minnesota 55439.
Copyright © 2017 by Abdo Consulting Group, Inc. International copyrights reserved in all countries. No part of this book may be reproduced in any form without written permission from the publisher. Big Buddy Books™ is a trademark and logo of Abdo Publishing.

Printed in the United States of America, North Mankato, Minnesota
062016
092016

THIS BOOK CONTAINS
RECYCLED MATERIALS

Design: Sarah DeYoung, Mighty Media, Inc.
Production: Mighty Media, Inc.
Editor: Rebecca Felix
Cover Photograph: LBJ Library/Museum
Interior Photographs: AP Images (pp. 13, 15, 17); LBJ Library (pp. 6, 7, 9, 11, 19, 21, 23, 25, 27, 29);
    LBJ Library/Frank Muto (p. 5)

Cataloging-in-Publication Data

Names: Gunderson, Megan M., author.
Title: Lyndon B. Johnson / by Megan M. Gunderson.
Description: Minneapolis, MN : Abdo Publishing, [2017] | Series: United States
    presidents | Includes bibliographical references and index.
Identifiers: LCCN 2015957546 | ISBN 9781680781045 (lib. bdg.) |
    ISBN 9781680775242 (ebook)
Subjects: LCSH: Johnson, Lyndon B. (Lyndon Baines), 1908-1973--Juvenile
    literature. | Presidents--United States--Biography--Juvenile literature. |
    United States--Politics and government--1963-1969--Juvenile literature.
Classification: DDC 973.923/092 [B]--dc23
LC record available at http://lccn.loc.gov/2015957546

Contents

Lyndon B. Johnson

On November 22, 1963, Lyndon B. Johnson became the thirty-sixth US president. He was **inaugurated** on the presidential airplane, Air Force One. It was unlike any other inauguration.

Less than two hours earlier, President John F. Kennedy had died. He had been shot while riding through Dallas, Texas.

As president, Johnson carried out many of Kennedy's plans for the nation. His popularity rose. In 1964, Americans elected Johnson to a full term.

Timeline

1908

On August 27, Lyndon Baines Johnson was born near Stonewall, Texas.

1937

Johnson was elected to the US House of **Representatives**.

1934

Johnson married Claudia Alta "Lady Bird" Taylor.

1948

Johnson was elected to the US Senate.

1963

President John F. Kennedy was killed on November 22. Johnson became president.

1973

On January 22, Lyndon B. Johnson died of a heart attack.

1960

Johnson was elected US vice president.

1964

On July 2, President Johnson signed the **Civil Rights** Act. In November, Johnson was elected for his full term.

7

Growing Up

Lyndon Baines Johnson was born near Stonewall, Texas, on August 27, 1908. He was the oldest of five children.

When Lyndon was five, his family moved to Johnson City, Texas. In school, Lyndon was known as a leader. He was class president.

★ FAST FACTS ★

Born: August 27, 1908

Wife: Claudia Alta "Lady Bird" Taylor (1912–2007)

Children: two

Political Party: Democrat

Age at Inauguration: 55

Years Served: 1963–1969

Vice President: Hubert H. Humphrey

Died: January 22, 1973, age 64

Lyndon's mother, Rebekah Baines Johnson, had been a teacher before she married.

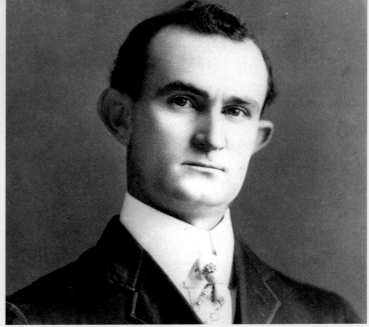

Lyndon's father, Samuel Ealy Johnson Jr., was a farmer and a schoolteacher. He also was a member of the Texas House of Representatives.

9

School and Family

In 1927, Johnson set out for college in San Marcos, Texas. He graduated in 1930. Soon, he went to Houston, Texas, and became a teacher.

Johnson also began helping with Texan Richard M. Kleberg's election campaign. Kleberg was elected to the US House of **Representatives**. Johnson became Kleberg's assistant.

In 1934, Johnson met Claudia Alta "Lady Bird" Taylor. They married within two months. The Johnsons had two daughters.

Claudia Alta "Lady Bird" Johnson (*far right*) and her husband with their daughters, Lynda (*lower left*) and Luci (*upper left*)

Young Politician

In 1935, Johnson became director of the National Youth **Administration** in Texas. The program gave jobs to students. That way, they could pay for school.

Johnson was elected to the US House of **Representatives** in 1937. He was also a member of the House Naval Affairs Committee. He felt strongly about preparing the US Navy for war.

In 1941, the United States entered **World War II**. Johnson served in the navy. He was the first congressman to serve on active duty in the war.

During World War II, Johnson served in the Pacific. He was given the Silver Star medal for bravery.

Johnson served 12 years in the US House of **Representatives**. Then, in 1948, he ran for the US Senate. Johnson won! He served in the Senate for 12 years.

Johnson soon became a **Democratic** Party leader. In 1955, he became **majority leader**. He was the youngest person to hold this title in Senate history.

In 1957 and 1960, Johnson helped pass two **civil rights** bills. Both bills concerned voting rights. They were the first civil rights bills passed in more than 80 years.

Johnson first ran for the US Senate in 1941. That year, he lost by just 1,311 votes! He went on to win in 1948, 1954, and 1960.

Vice President

In 1960, the **Democrats** chose John F. Kennedy to run for president. They chose Johnson as Kennedy's **running mate**. Kennedy and Johnson won the election. Johnson became vice president.

Johnson was an active vice president. He attended **cabinet**, national security, and other White House meetings. He was also head of the President's Committee on Equal Employment Opportunity. This group focused on ending racial **discrimination** when hiring workers.

On July 13, 1960, the Democrats chose Kennedy (*far right*) to run for president. The following day, Johnson (*far left*) was chosen to run for vice president.

In 1963, Kennedy, Johnson, and their wives traveled to Texas. On November 22, Kennedy and Johnson rode through downtown Dallas. Kennedy was in the backseat of one car. Johnson was two cars behind him.

Suddenly, gunshots rang out. President Kennedy was hit. He was rushed to the hospital where he died.

Later that day, Johnson boarded Air Force One to return to Washington, DC. He was **inaugurated** on the airplane. He became the thirty-sixth US president.

Mrs. Johnson (*left*) and Mrs. Kennedy (*right*) stood by Johnson's side as he was inaugurated.

President Johnson

In the weeks following Kennedy's death, Johnson showed strong leadership. He helped calm the nation. President Johnson also worked with Congress to pass important laws.

On July 2, 1964, Johnson signed the **Civil Rights** Act. It banned **discrimination** in public places. And, it promised equal voting rights.

As president, Johnson worked to continue Kennedy's plans. He worked on laws that would help the poor and **support** education. He also signed a large tax cut.

President Johnson signing
the Civil Rights Act of 1964

Meanwhile, there was trouble in Asia. Back in 1954, Vietnam had split in two. The North and South held different **political** beliefs.

Elections were planned for 1956 to **reunite** the countries. But South Vietnam's leader refused to take part in the elections. Then North Vietnam attacked South Vietnam.

The United States became involved in the **conflict**. It became known as the **Vietnam War**. Johnson sent American troops to fight.

★ SUPREME COURT ★ APPOINTMENTS

Abe Fortas: 1965

Thurgood Marshall: 1967

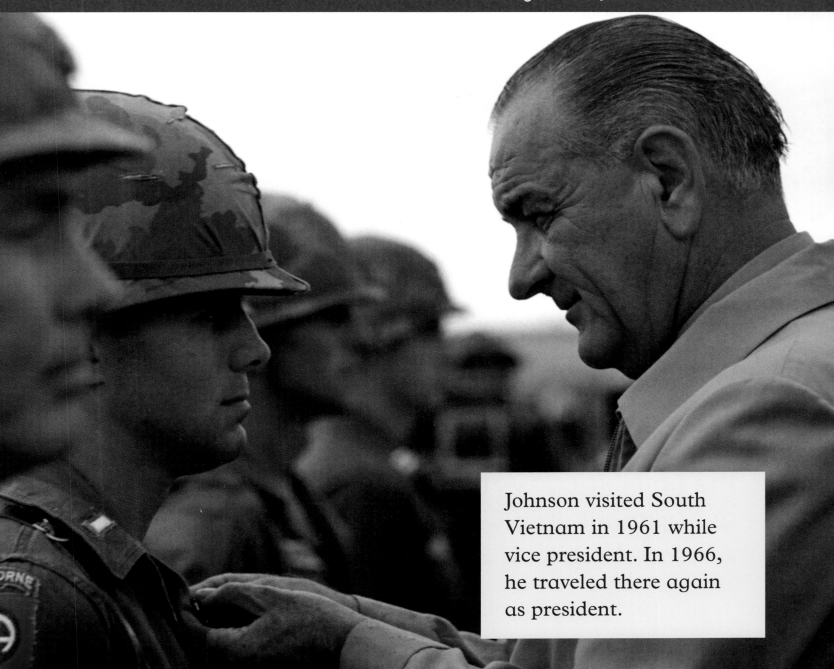

Johnson visited South Vietnam in 1961 while vice president. In 1966, he traveled there again as president.

Civil Rights

On November 3, 1964, Johnson was elected president. His **running mate** was Minnesota senator Hubert H. Humphrey. Johnson began his first full term on January 20, 1965.

President Johnson continued to fight for **civil rights**. He signed the Voting Rights Act in 1965. In 1966, he named Robert C. Weaver the first African-American head of a **cabinet** department. In 1967, Johnson named the first African-American **Supreme Court justice**.

Johnson (*right*) with the first African-American Supreme Court justice, Thurgood Marshall (*left*)

Meanwhile, the **Vietnam War** was going badly. President Johnson sent more and more troops to help South Vietnam. Many soldiers died in the war. At home, many Americans spoke out against the war. Johnson's popularity fell quickly.

By 1968, many Americans felt the war would not end soon. On March 31, Johnson announced a reduction in attacks on North Vietnam. And, he suggested the opening of peace talks. Johnson also stated that he would not run for reelection.

PRESIDENT JOHNSON'S CABINET

First Term
November 22, 1963–January 20, 1965

★ **STATE:** Dean Rusk

★ **TREASURY:** C. Douglas Dillon

★ **DEFENSE:** Robert S. McNamara

★ **ATTORNEY GENERAL:** Robert F. Kennedy

★ **INTERIOR:** Stewart L. Udall

★ **AGRICULTURE:** Orville L. Freeman

★ **COMMERCE:** Luther H. Hodges

★ **LABOR:** W. Willard Wirtz

★ **HEALTH, EDUCATION, AND WELFARE:**
Anthony J. Celebrezze

Second Term
January 20, 1965–January 20, 1969

★ **STATE:** Dean Rusk

★ **TREASURY:** C. Douglas Dillon,
Henry H. Fowler (from April 1, 1965),
Joseph W. Barr (from December 23, 1968)

★ **DEFENSE:** Robert S. McNamara,
Clark M. Clifford (from March 1, 1968)

★ **ATTORNEY GENERAL:**
Nicholas deBelleville Katzenbach,
Ramsey Clark (from March 10, 1967)

★ **INTERIOR:** Stewart L. Udall

★ **AGRICULTURE:** Orville L. Freeman

★ **COMMERCE:** John T. Connor,
Alexander B. Trowbridge (from June 14, 1967),
C.R. Smith (from March 6, 1968)

★ **LABOR:** W. Willard Wirtz

★ **HEALTH, EDUCATION, AND WELFARE:**
Anthony J. Celebrezze,
John William Gardner (from August 18, 1965),
Wilbur J. Cohen (from May 9, 1968)

★ **HOUSING AND URBAN DEVELOPMENT:**
Robert C. Weaver (from January 18, 1966),
Robert Coldwell Wood (from January 7, 1969)

★ **TRANSPORTATION:**
Alan S. Boyd (from January 16, 1967)

After Politics

January 20, 1969, was Johnson's last day as president. The Johnsons lived on the LBJ Ranch. It is near Johnson City.

In 1971, the Lyndon Baines Johnson Library and Museum was opened to public use. It is located at the University of Texas at Austin.

On January 22, 1973, Lyndon B. Johnson died of a heart attack. He was a congressman, a senator, and a president. As president, Johnson showed strong leadership. In every office, he worked hard to serve his country.

Johnson wanted the Lyndon Baines Johnson Library and Museum to help visitors better understand the presidency.

Office of the President

Branches of Government

The US government has three branches. They are the executive, legislative, and judicial branches. Each branch has some power over the others. This is called a system of checks and balances.

★ Executive Branch

The executive branch enforces laws. It is made up of the president, the vice president, and the president's cabinet. The president represents the United States around the world. He or she also signs bills into law and leads the military.

★ Legislative Branch

The legislative branch makes laws, maintains the military, and regulates trade. It also has the power to declare war. This branch includes the Senate and the House of Representatives. Together, these two houses form Congress.

★ Judicial Branch

The judicial branch interprets laws. It is made up of district courts, courts of appeals, and the Supreme Court. District courts try cases. Sometimes people disagree with a trial's outcome. Then he or she may appeal. If a court of appeals supports the ruling, a person may appeal to the Supreme Court.

Qualifications for Office

To be president, a candidate must be at least 35 years old. The person must be a natural-born US citizen. He or she must also have lived in the United States for at least 14 years.

Electoral College

The US presidential election is an indirect election. Voters from each state choose electors. These electors represent their state in the Electoral College. Each elector has one electoral vote. Electors cast their vote for the candidate with the highest number of votes from people in their state. A candidate must receive the majority of Electoral College votes to win.

Term of Office

Each president may be elected to two four-year terms. The presidential election is held on the Tuesday after the first Monday in November. The president is sworn in on January 20 of the following year. At that time, he or she takes the oath of office.
It states:

I do solemnly swear (or affirm) that I will faithfully execute the office of President of the United States, and will to the best of my ability, preserve, protect and defend the Constitution of the United States.

31

Line of Succession

The Presidential Succession Act of 1947 states who becomes president if the president cannot serve. The vice president is first in the line. Next are the Speaker of the House and the President Pro Tempore of the Senate. It may happen that none of these individuals is able to serve. Then the office falls to the president's cabinet members. They would take office in the order in which each department was created:

Secretary of State

Secretary of the Treasury

Secretary of Defense

Attorney General

Secretary of the Interior

Secretary of Agriculture

Secretary of Commerce

Secretary of Labor

Secretary of Health and Human Services

Secretary of Housing and Urban Development

Secretary of Transportation

Secretary of Energy

Secretary of Education

Secretary of Veterans Affairs

Secretary of Homeland Security

Benefits

★ While in office, the president receives a salary. It is $400,000 per year. He or she lives in the White House. The president also has 24-hour Secret Service protection.

★ The president may travel on a Boeing 747 jet. This special jet is called Air Force One. It can hold 70 passengers. It has kitchens, a dining room, sleeping areas, and more. Air Force One can fly halfway around the world before needing to refuel. It can even refuel in flight!

★ When the president travels by car, he or she uses Cadillac One. It is a Cadillac Deville that has been modified. The car has heavy armor and communications systems. The president may even take Cadillac One along when visiting other countries.

★ The president also travels on a helicopter. It is called Marine One. It may also be taken along when the president visits other countries.

★ Sometimes the president needs to get away with family and friends. Camp David is the official presidential retreat. It is located in Maryland. The US Navy maintains the retreat. The US Marine Corps keeps it secure. The camp offers swimming, tennis, golf, and hiking.

★ When the president leaves office, he or she receives lifetime Secret Service protection. He or she also receives a yearly pension of $203,700. The former president also receives money for office space, supplies, and staff.

PRESIDENTS AND THEIR TERMS

PRESIDENT	PARTY	TOOK OFFICE	LEFT OFFICE	TERMS SERVED	VICE PRESIDENT
George Washington	None	April 30, 1789	March 4, 1797	Two	John Adams
John Adams	Federalist	March 4, 1797	March 4, 1801	One	Thomas Jefferson
Thomas Jefferson	Democratic-Republican	March 4, 1801	March 4, 1809	Two	Aaron Burr, George Clinton
James Madison	Democratic-Republican	March 4, 1809	March 4, 1817	Two	George Clinton, Elbridge Gerry
James Monroe	Democratic-Republican	March 4, 1817	March 4, 1825	Two	Daniel D. Tompkins
John Quincy Adams	Democratic-Republican	March 4, 1825	March 4, 1829	One	John C. Calhoun
Andrew Jackson	Democrat	March 4, 1829	March 4, 1837	Two	John C. Calhoun, Martin Van Buren
Martin Van Buren	Democrat	March 4, 1837	March 4, 1841	One	Richard M. Johnson
William H. Harrison	Whig	March 4, 1841	April 4, 1841	Died During First Term	John Tyler
John Tyler	Whig	April 6, 1841	March 4, 1845	Completed Harrison's Term	Office Vacant
James K. Polk	Democrat	March 4, 1845	March 4, 1849	One	George M. Dallas
Zachary Taylor	Whig	March 5, 1849	July 9, 1850	Died During First Term	Millard Fillmore

PRESIDENT	PARTY	TOOK OFFICE	LEFT OFFICE	TERMS SERVED	VICE PRESIDENT
Millard Fillmore	Whig	July 10, 1850	March 4, 1853	Completed Taylor's Term	Office Vacant
Franklin Pierce	Democrat	March 4, 1853	March 4, 1857	One	William R.D. King
James Buchanan	Democrat	March 4, 1857	March 4, 1861	One	John C. Breckinridge
Abraham Lincoln	Republican	March 4, 1861	April 15, 1865	Served One Term, Died During Second Term	Hannibal Hamlin, Andrew Johnson
Andrew Johnson	Democrat	April 15, 1865	March 4, 1869	Completed Lincoln's Second Term	Office Vacant
Ulysses S. Grant	Republican	March 4, 1869	March 4, 1877	Two	Schuyler Colfax, Henry Wilson
Rutherford B. Hayes	Republican	March 3, 1877	March 4, 1881	One	William A. Wheeler
James A. Garfield	Republican	March 4, 1881	September 19, 1881	Died During First Term	Chester Arthur
Chester Arthur	Republican	September 20, 1881	March 4, 1885	Completed Garfield's Term	Office Vacant
Grover Cleveland	Democrat	March 4, 1885	March 4, 1889	One	Thomas A. Hendricks
Benjamin Harrison	Republican	March 4, 1889	March 4, 1893	One	Levi P. Morton
Grover Cleveland	Democrat	March 4, 1893	March 4, 1897	One	Adlai E. Stevenson
William McKinley	Republican	March 4, 1897	September 14, 1901	Served One Term, Died During Second Term	Garret A. Hobart, Theodore Roosevelt

PRESIDENT	PARTY	TOOK OFFICE	LEFT OFFICE	TERMS SERVED	VICE PRESIDENT
Theodore Roosevelt	Republican	September 14, 1901	March 4, 1909	Completed McKinley's Second Term, Served One Term	Office Vacant, Charles Fairbanks
William Taft	Republican	March 4, 1909	March 4, 1913	One	James S. Sherman
Woodrow Wilson	Democrat	March 4, 1913	March 4, 1921	Two	Thomas R. Marshall
Warren G. Harding	Republican	March 4, 1921	August 2, 1923	Died During First Term	Calvin Coolidge
Calvin Coolidge	Republican	August 3, 1923	March 4, 1929	Completed Harding's Term, Served One Term	Office Vacant, Charles Dawes
Herbert Hoover	Republican	March 4, 1929	March 4, 1933	One	Charles Curtis
Franklin D. Roosevelt	Democrat	March 4, 1933	April 12, 1945	Served Three Terms, Died During Fourth Term	John Nance Garner, Henry A. Wallace, Harry S. Truman
Harry S. Truman	Democrat	April 12, 1945	January 20, 1953	Completed Roosevelt's Fourth Term, Served One Term	Office Vacant, Alben Barkley
Dwight D. Eisenhower	Republican	January 20, 1953	January 20, 1961	Two	Richard Nixon
John F. Kennedy	Democrat	January 20, 1961	November 22, 1963	Died During First Term	Lyndon B. Johnson
Lyndon B. Johnson	Democrat	November 22, 1963	January 20, 1969	Completed Kennedy's Term, Served One Term	Office Vacant, Hubert H. Humphrey
Richard Nixon	Republican	January 20, 1969	August 9, 1974	Completed First Term, Resigned During Second Term	Spiro T. Agnew, Gerald Ford

PRESIDENT	PARTY	TOOK OFFICE	LEFT OFFICE	TERMS SERVED	VICE PRESIDENT
Gerald Ford	Republican	August 9, 1974	January 20, 1977	Completed Nixon's Second Term	Nelson A. Rockefeller
Jimmy Carter	Democrat	January 20, 1977	January 20, 1981	One	Walter Mondale
Ronald Reagan	Republican	January 20, 1981	January 20, 1989	Two	George H.W. Bush
George H.W. Bush	Republican	January 20, 1989	January 20, 1993	One	Dan Quayle
Bill Clinton	Democrat	January 20, 1993	January 20, 2001	Two	Al Gore
George W. Bush	Republican	January 20, 2001	January 20, 2009	Two	Dick Cheney
Barack Obama	Democrat	January 20, 2009	January 20, 2017	Two	Joe Biden

"A President's hardest task is not to do what is right, but to know what is right."

Lyndon B. Johnson

★ WRITE TO THE PRESIDENT ★

You may write to the president at:
The White House
1600 Pennsylvania Avenue NW
Washington, DC 20500

You may e-mail the president at:
comments@whitehouse.gov

37

Glossary

administration (uhd-mih-nuh-STRAY-shuhn)—a group of people that manages an operation, a department, or an office.

cabinet—a group of advisers chosen by the president to lead government departments.

civil rights—the rights of a citizen, such as the right to vote or freedom of speech.

conflict—strong disagreement between people or groups.

Democrat—a member of the Democratic political party.

discrimination—the treating of some people better than others without any fair or proper reason.

inaugurate—to swear into a political office.

justice—a judge on the US Supreme Court.

majority leader—the leader of the party that has the greatest number of votes in a legislative body, such as the US Senate.

politics—the art or science of government. Something referring to politics is political. A person who is active in politics is a politician.

representative—someone chosen in an election to act or speak for the people who voted for him or her.

reunite—to bring together again.

running mate—someone running for vice president with another person running for president in an election.

support—to provide money for.

Supreme Court—the highest, most powerful court of a nation or a state.

Vietnam War—a war that took place between South Vietnam and North Vietnam from 1957 to 1975. The United States was involved in this war for many years.

World War II—a war fought in Europe, Asia, and Africa from 1939 to 1945.

★ WEBSITES ★

To learn more about the US Presidents, visit **booklinks.abdopublishing.com**. These links are routinely monitored and updated to provide the most current information available.

Index